The Royal Observer
Corps in Worthing

This publication follows the history of the Royal Observer Corps in
Worthing, West Sussex, from the days of identifying enemy aircraft,
right through to their new, rather chilling role, trained to monitor a
nuclear attack on Britain from the confines of an underground
bunker on the Worthing / Lancing border.

Graham Lelliott

The Royal Observer Corps in Worthing

© Copyright Graham Lelliott, 2008.

10 Digit ISBN 0-9553893-3-X
13 Digit ISBN 978-0-9553893-3-7

Published by;
Graham Lelliott, 3 Busticle Lane, Sompting,
Lancing, West Sussex, BN15 0DH, England
Website: www.grahamlelliott.co.uk

Printed and bound in 2008 by;
CPI Antony Rowe, 48-50 Birch Close,
Eastbourne, East Sussex, BN23 6PE, England
Tel: + 44 (0)1323 434700
Website: www.antonyrowe.co.uk

This book is dedicated to all who served
in the Royal Observer Corps.

(Crown Copyright / Ministry of Defence)

Contents

Introduction

Until July 2007, I was completely unaware of the Royal Observer Corps. It was not until I visited Newhaven Fort in East Sussex, that I was able to learn about their role. With thanks to the Royal Observer Corps Historic Collection, a wonderful display had been put together and I feel if it had not been for this visit I may well have never learnt about the existence of the Corps.

Many towns and villages had a Royal Observer Corps presence for many years, Worthing being no exception. Still having book projects in the pipeline, this subject had become a priority to discover more about the Corps in Worthing. I suddenly realised that a new book project had begun.

To ensure that the reader understands what role the Corps played and why they were present in Worthing, I feel it has been necessary to include a general history of the Corps from its origins, right through to its stand down in 1992. This is not however a definitive history.

It has been almost impossible to obtain photographs of the Corps in Worthing, so on some occasions it has been necessary to use other photographs of other areas. All photographs, diagrams and other sources used have been acknowledged and copyright permission granted. However if something has been overlooked, then this is down to human error and is completely unintentional.

Graham Lelliott

The History of the Corps in Worthing

The origins of the Royal Observer Corps can be traced right back to 1915. During 1915 Zeppelin airships were becoming an increasing problem for Britain. Air defences in Britain at this time was virtually non-existant. The country could only rely upon information given by the police, Army units, gun positions and even railway stations. By the time the information had been passed on to "Anti Aircraft London" and the correct reporting procedures followed, it was quite likely that enemy had by now returned home.

When the War Office took over in 1916 there was some improvement. They had installed many searchlight posts stretching from Sussex to Northumberland, although the observation system was later re-organised with 200 observation posts established.

These observation posts proved to be successful in combating the Zeppelin although by now biplane bombers, such as the Gotha and the Staken Giant were now Britain's main threat. On 13th June 1917, twenty Gothas made a daylight raid on London. The bombing was fairly severe however surprisingly there were no casualties.

This incident provoked a public outcry and the Government's reaction was to put all ground and air defence of London under the command of one officer. The man chosen for this task was Major General E. B. Ashmore, who would be officially acknowledged by the War Office on 31st July 1917 as the London Air Defence Area (LADA).

He immediately began dealing with day raids and changed the current troops on observation duties to policemen. Reports of enemy aircraft would be phoned through to LADA Central Control at the Horse Guards London and the British aircraft controlled from there. This proved to be a success and Germany halted low level daylight raids, although they would now begin operating at night or above 10,000 ft.

In August and September of 1924 Major General Ashmore carried out observing and plotting experiments with assistance from Special Constables. From this, two counties, Kent and Sussex, were to be given temporary controls, or operations rooms, in both. Ashmore wrote to two Chief Constables asking for Special Constables to be made available or enrolled to man 44 posts in two groups and made it clear that their purpose would remain secret.

Major General E. B. Ashmore.
(Crown Copyright / Ministry of Defence)

A photograph of a wooden post instrument, which was used during the 1920's and early 1930's. Binoculars, a telephone battery box and army type head and breast set can also be seen.
(The Royal Observer Corps Historic Collection)

Due to the success of the observing and plotting experiments carried out in August and September of 1924, on the 8th July 1925 recommendations were made to extend the observer network to Hampshire and Essex in order to protect London from enemy aircraft flying in from the continent. The Committee of Imperial Defence approved the scheme on 29th October 1925.

The Observer Corps may have been able to trace its foundation back to the First World War, however the official month of inauguration of the corps would be October 1925.

Terms and conditions were laid down, one of these being that; "The Observer Corps shall consist of volunteers, enrolled as Special Constables, who undertake to carry out observation work in the air defence of Great Britain as part of their constabulary duties."

By 1928 suggestions had been made to extend the cover throughout the country and owing to the success of the Observer Corps, responsibility was passed on from the War Office to the Air Ministry, thus becoming part of the Royal Air Force. The following year, Observer Corps founder, Major General E. B. Ashmore decided it was time to retire.

Worthing's observer post opened that same year (1929) and was located on the roof of the pavilion at the southern end of the corporation's pier. Known as 2/N.4, its location was considered to be the ideal place to spot enemy aircraft.

Not much is known about the early days of the Observer Corps in Worthing, although it had been noted that in the early hours of the 20th July 1931, Worthing's post participated in a 24-hour top-secret military exercise in which Royal Air Force biplanes acted as the enemy as they continued to fly over the town.

By the time the sun had risen many Worthing residents were discussing the number of aircraft that had flown over the town during the hours of darkness. Some of them even complained to the police and to the Town Hall about the noise, which was agreed by many as ear deafening at times.

A Worthing Herald reporter had already received reports of light signals seen during the early hours, which were being flashed occasionally from the end of the pier. The reporter decided to investigate so he wondered along the pier and climbed a ladder leaning against the southern pavilion.

His actions were soon terminated by the firm response of "only officials allowed." The reporter's investigation had not got very far, however within the hour his "sources" had discovered that Worthing was "one of a circle of stations from which information about the whereabouts of enemy aircraft was being supplied."

A letter, titled "Noisy aircraft at night", was later published in the Worthing Herald and explained; "Sir, I should like to make a strong protest against the discordant noise caused by the droning of aeroplanes over the town until midnight, thereby disturbing invalid and elderly persons. Surely 10pm is quite late enough for them to cease when they have been carrying on all day. There are a large amount of visitors in the town who come here for rest and quiet, to escape from the noise and din of the large towns."

It was not until after World War Two that Worthing eventually found out what had actually gone on that particular day. Harold Bird, director of Wades car dealership came forward and explained in detail the part he had played in the exercise on the end of Worthing pier. He suspected that he was now the last surviving special constable who had taken part in the 1931 exercise.

He recalled; "I had become a special at the time of the general strike, when police were extremely under manned. You were supposed to be 21 years old to qualify but they let me in at the age of 17. I was sworn in at the Town Hall and within an hour was on the streets of Worthing complete with truncheon and armband. Everyone was very kind and even occasional traffic duty was quite civilised at that time.

I remember the so-called technical equipment that was installed at the southern pavilion on that occasion, for the tracking of 'enemy' aircraft. It comprised a table covered with a mat, on top of which was a grid map to allow aircraft to be plotted. There was also a calibrated height bar to estimate how high planes were flying.

We worked in teams of four with the aim of making visual sightings of aircraft, estimate their height and contact the chief control centre at Horsham, which would then try to track and "fix" the aircraft. Unfortunately, my Worthing colleagues were three Boer War veterans who could not see too well and whose hearing was far from perfect. There were occasions when there was a grave risk of us plotting seagulls or passing motorbikes, for, with a high wind blowing, it was difficult to identify sounds!"

Harold Bird recalls that reports at the time of the number of aircraft taking part in the exercise had been grossly exaggerated. He explained; "Very few aircraft were involved. There might have been three in an hour but the average was nearer one an hour. In the event of an aircraft flying directly overhead, we would also contact tracking stations at Arundel and Steyning which would then hopefully make a visual sighting of the plane – despite the Downs in between – and the aircraft's speed and direction could be calculated. Because of the country's very low state of readiness for war in 1931, the aircraft involved were all slow and cumbersome biplanes."

As for the contemporary reports of light signals being flashed occasionally during the 1931 exercise, Harold Bird recalled; "The only flashing that went on was by the older members of the squad trying to find their way around the pier in the darkness. As the youngest member of the southern pavilion spotter team, I didn't even have to stay on duty all night. The others sent me home early while they stayed on – to escape from their wives!"

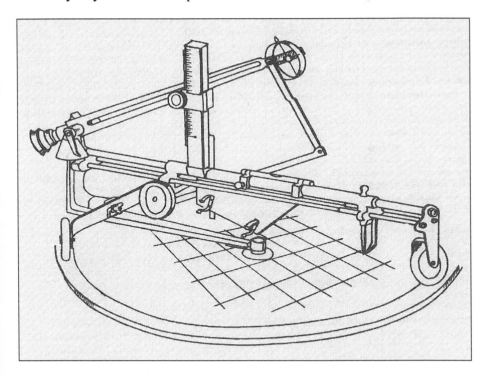

A diagram of the post instrument issued in 1935, used to identify the enemy's height and course. (The National Archives)

In May 1939 the observation post on the roof of the south pavilion was renamed to 2/N.3. Notes on this post were made on 22nd April 1940, which explained; "Post 2/N.3 Worthing 22/4/40 – Have just completed glass sided hut, but has only been made with overlapping weather board and badly needs lining. O.G.O has allotted £5 towards cost but it will be much nearer £8 without lining.

Put up special case with C.O.C to provide for lining owing to exposed position out on pier, and because they have not been provided with a standard hut. Access to roof very bad being builders ladder with no guys or rails. Get O.G.O to take up for provision of a ships gangway or brow, which could be used instead, facing south, and rope handrails provided to flagstaff."

In June 1940 the post was relocated to the roof of the County Restaurant, Marine Parade. All equipment, including the wooden hut was dismantled and re-erected at the new site. The purpose of relocating was down to the pier being "sectioned". Just like all other piers in the country, a large hole was blown in the pier to prevent it being used as a possible landing stage in the event of an invasion.

By 1938 the Munich crisis had emphasised the need for effective air defences and by 1934 the corps had began to spread across Britain. Posts were organised into clusters of two to four posts, reporting to Group Centres, which passed on the information through Fighter Group and Sector Operations Rooms up to Fighter Command.

The Second World War broke out in 1939 and thankfully by now, most of mainland Britain was covered by the Observer Corps, however south west Scotland, the Highlands, western Wales and Cornwall, were very poorly equipped. Surprisingly Northern Island and the Isle of Man had no Observer posts at all.

The next few years would test their skills to the limit as the Luftwaffe continued to fly over the English Channel to try and destroy villages, towns, cities, airfields, etc. Many radar stations would be targeted, meaning the Observer Corp would obviously be relied upon even more. The Battle of Britain and the Blitz proved to be the most pressing times for the Observer Corps during the Second World War. During this time, blue RAF overalls, berets and identity cards were issued, although many preferred to remain in civilian clothes as some said the overalls looked awful and did not fit properly.

Their hard work had not gone unnoticed. On 9th April 1941 His Majesty King George VI acknowledged their efforts and professionalism and changed their title to the "Royal Observer Corps".

This royal link was later passed onto Her Majesty Queen Elizabeth II who continued with being patron of the Corps. Subsequently, new uniform was once again supplied, along with new badges.

To give the reader some idea of how hectic 2/N.3 Worthing post was during wartime, entries from just two days in August have been extracted from the 1942 Worthing logbook and are as follows;

"12th August
04.00 – 21 Wellingtons and four engined bombers south.
05.44 – Air raid warning.
05.49 – Two Fw190s seen 5917 south at zero. Turned west. Underneath of wings appeared yellow. N.2 reports two Fw190s attacked Lysander on 3711. Lysander successfully evaded and returned to Shoreham with two holes in wing and one in fuselage.
06.02 – Two Fw190s seen west on 6323 at zero. Guns on pier fired as aircraft approached and passed end of pier. Smith fired four rounds with post rifle. Machine turned out on 5921 and went SE at full throttle. Last plot 6113. (These two machines had also attacked a Lysander off Newhaven.) Under surfaces of wings and fuselage of the two Fw190s were painted yellow.
12.08 – Message from duty controller congratulating crew on duty at N.3, 11.8.42, on recognition of Swordfish in distress. Plane landed safely mainly due to their plotting. Landed at Thorney.

19th August
(This was the day of the abortive allied landings at Dieppe)
04.40 – Large numbers of fighters, accompanied by Beauforts, Blenheims and Bostons, out in raid to Dieppe.
05.25 – Fighters and bombers started to return.
05.44 – Two Fw190s on 5719 going east at 50ft. Zoomed to 2,500ft on 6121.
05.45 – Red alert rung.
05.46 – Boston coming from east attacked on 6121 by the two Fw190s, which dived on it and attacked from above and rear on starboard and port sides. Boston immediately burst into flames crash landed in sea on 5919 and sank immediately. Spitfire north of post flying east to west turned and engaged hostile aircraft. After exchange of cannon fire, Spitfire collided with one

- 9 -

Fw190 while making a vertical diving turn to port. Both machines broke to pieces in the air and crashed in flames. Hurricane had also joined in the fight. Remaining Fw190 broke off engagement and went out SE. Hurricane went away west.

06.20 – Walrus and two Spitfires searching in 5919. Crash boat reached scene from Littlehampton at 06.30 and was seen to pick up four white objects (bodies).

10.05 – 24 Fortresses.

10.55 – 24 Hurricanes, 12 with bombs, 24 Spitfires.

10.56 – News from centre; all fortresses returned to Maidstone area.

11.17 – 65 Hurricanes, and Spitfires returned.

11.26 – 6 Bostons (+36 Hurricanes and Spitfires) sweep and 12 Hurricanes (Shoreham).

11.30 – 6 Bostons, 12 fighters.

11.42 – 20 return; 4 Bostons,

12.00 – 12 Bostons and 48 Spitfires.

12.20 – Return from sweep. 11 Bostons, three Blenheims, eight fighters.

12.59 – Six Hurribombers east.

13.00 – 11 Spitfires, six Bostons east 5909.

13.25 – Ten Hurribombers, 12 Spits southeast; 16 Spits, six Bostons west.

14.00 – 24 Spits east.

14.30 – 12 Spits SE.

14.43 – Nine Hurribombers west.

14.45 – 11 Hurricanes west.

14.53 – 23 Hurries and Spits west.

14.55 – 66 fighters SE.

15.00 – Three Spits west.

15.32 – Air raid warning.

15.51 – 20 fighters west.

15.57 – Air raid warning.

16.37 – Local alarm. Convoy of barges attacked by hostile planes on 6117, at least one barge sunk. Four Fw190s.

17.32 – Alarm Worthing.

18.19 – Very heavy explosion.

18.29 – Alarm Worthing.

18.40 – Ju88 plotted SE on 6319.

19.52 – Alarm Worthing. Two Fw190s east on 5919, 50ft. Pier opened fire."

In May 1943, Worthing's Post was renamed to 2/S.3, although remained on the roof of the County Restaurant in Marine Parade.

A wartime photograph showing the new Royal Observer
Corps uniform and instrumentation issued in 1935.
(The Royal Observer Corps Historic Collection)

Preparations for D-day later took place and the Royal Observer Corps was
approached and asked to volunteer for service aboard naval ships for 6th June
1944. Known as Seaborne Observers, over 700 individuals would take part.

Worthing, Littlehampton and Bognor would be used as rendezvous points for
the 6th Airborne Division, before flying out over the English Channel to
Normandy.

Worthing Observer Corps would witness glider towing tugs and paratrooper
transporters, flown from airfields in Oxfordshire, Berkshire, Wiltshire and
Dorset.

A wartime photograph showing three observers at work.
(The Royal Observer Corps Historic Collection)

The Second World War ended the following year, however while everyone took part in the VE-day celebrations the Royal Observer Corps remained at their posts in fear of renegade Luftwaffe units attacking the country. The Corps stood down at 17:00 on 12th May 1945.

By November 1945 Air Commodore (later Air Chief Marshal) The Earl of Bandon would be responsible for laying down foundations for a post war Royal Observer Corps. He would face many months without any officially announced policy for re-organisation and at the time only employed 230 men and women.

No centres were operationally in use and there were only a few cluster meetings for posts to attend. I understand some posts kept their own meetings regardless but even so there was no official training syllabus.

It was noted that on 7th September 1946, observers were supplied from Worthing (2/S.3) and Middleton posts (2/N.2), to give warning of the approach of Royal Air Force High-Speed Flight Meteors along the south coast course. It was on this day Group Captain E. M Donaldson broke a new world air speed record of 615.78 m.p.h.

A new royal warrant was prepared for the corps and on the 15th November 1946, the commandant sent out letters to all wartime observers who had shown an interest in joining the peacetime Royal Observer Corps. With training commencing on 1st January 1947, the corps was now very much back in active service.

Many previous posts on top of buildings had been vandalised or had become dilapidated. Some of the buildings themselves had been derequisitioned and handed back to civilian owners, although Worthing Royal Observer Corps volunteers returned to the roof of the County Restaurant in Marine Parade.

Many posts however had new prefabricated concrete posts built by the Orlit Company. These measured roughly 11ft by 8ft and were built on a simple concrete base. Part of the post was undercover, with the remainder being open, to be able to identify enemy aircraft. A concrete plinth was located in the middle to accommodate the map and instrumentation. The Mark II version was mounted on concrete stilts, although this was mainly used on flat land.

In November 1953 Worthing's post was once again renamed. This was changed to 2/E.2 and continued to be located on the roof of the County Restaurant in Marine Parade.

The Royal Observer Corp was expanded in 1955 to cover Northern Ireland and parts of northwest Scotland. Russia's nuclear research was beginning to bother the British Government and by having these posts, ROC volunteers would be able to monitor Russian aircraft such as the long-range tupolev "Bear" bomber.

In 1957 the Observers began to take on an additional task. This rather sinister and chilling role would be to measure and report the onset, location and after effects of a possible nuclear attack from the Soviet Union. The Royal Observer Corps had in the past reported to the Royal Air Force, however this would change to Group and Sector Controls now run by the officials and scientists of the United Kingdom Warning and Monitoring Organisation.

The UKWMO (a service run by the Home Office) would be responsible for identifying and giving the warning of an air attack, then assessing and advising the effects of a possible nuclear, chemical or biological weapons attack. The nuclear role was the most developed and considered the most credible. As a result of this, the Royal Observer Corps volunteers would be required to learn and know how to operate, much more instrumentation than ever before.

Due to the incredible power of a nuclear blast, followed by the effects of lethal radiation, the Corps would also require some sort of protection. Between 1957 and 1964 observers moved from rainy and windswept surface posts to 1,563 identical reinforced concrete underground monitoring posts, located throughout Great Britain and Northern Ireland.

Generally, the underground posts were constructed at the same location as the aircraft monitoring post, however this was not always possible. Worthing's post is a fine example of this.

Minutes for a Worthing Borough Council meeting held on 12th May 1959 stated the following; "Air Ministry-Royal Observer Corps Post-Brooklands. RESOLVED, that upon the report of the Borough Engineer, authority be given in principle to the establishment of an Air Ministry Royal Observer Corps post on land at Brooklands, so far as this committee is concerned."

Bunker construction began within the newly landscaped Brooklands Pleasure Park, close to the Worthing / Lancing border and was located on the higher ground overlooking the children's paddling pools.

The beginning of bunker construction is shown here. Steel reinforcing rods can be seen as well as the sump at the top right of the base. In the event of a flood, water in this sump would be pumped out using the hand pump fitted to the side of the entrance shaft. (The Royal Observer Corps Historic Collection)

Concrete is poured into the wooden "moulds" which are placed around the steel reinforcing rods. Once the concrete has set, these "moulds" are taken away. (The Royal Observer Corps Historic Collection)

Once complete, the outside is "tanked" with bitumen to ensure the bunker does not leak. The bunker is then covered with earth leaving only the entrance shaft and ventilation shaft visible. Two pipes also protrude for the Fixed Survey Meter and Bomb Power Indicator – the need for these will be explained later in this publication. (The Royal Observer Corps Historic Collection)

It is unknown how long bunker construction took to complete at Worthing, however the underground post opened in October 1961. Although geographically sited within the Borough of Worthing, it is unclear why the Royal Observer Corps changed the name to Lancing Post in October 1962.

Once inside the bunker, the monitoring room was often customised to suit individual needs, such as adding bedside curtains, comfy chairs and carpet. A ventilation shaft was located alongside the entrance shaft, with a second ventilation shaft at the other end of the room, just above the bunk beds. Both of these had steel shutters, which could be opened or closed.

Lighting consisted of a single bulb, although for many, this proved to be insufficient and so in many cases, a small strip light was also added. These were powered by a 12-volt battery, located behind the monitoring room door.

Part of a 1964 Worthing Borough Council plan of Brooklands Pleasure Park can be seen below. The unmarked square on the left of this image shows the site of the Lancing underground post, located on its own within the higher ground. Note the pleasure boat landing stage, pathways, proposed miniature railway and paddling pools in the shapes of a giraffe, elephant, rabbit and duck. A single paddling pool would later replace these. (Worthing Borough Council)

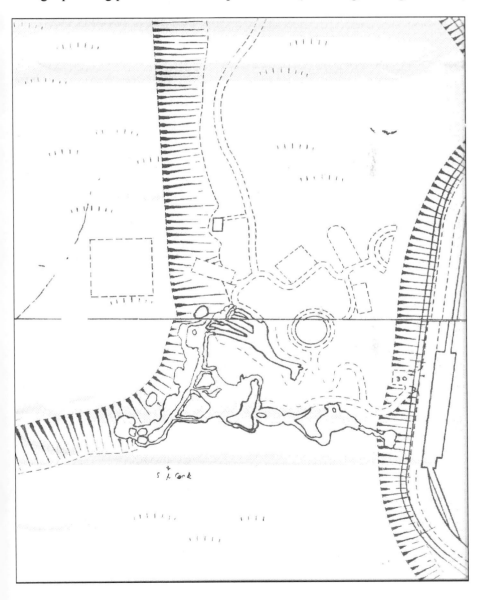

From this computer-generated image, one can see the overall layout of the 15 ft by 7 ft, 6 inch bunker, which consisted of a 15 ft vertical entrance shaft. This gave access to two rooms, one containing a chemical toilet and the other, a much larger monitoring room. The latter was furnished with canvas chairs, a folding table, a shelf, a small cupboard with two doors, and a pair of metal-framed bunk beds with mattresses. An additional single metal-framed bed was kept within the post, although these would often remain dismantled.
(Greg Smith)

Each post was fitted with several instruments, which would measure the explosive blast, the height and angle of the flash from the nuclear explosion and the lethal radiation from weapons fallout. These are described below.

The Fixed Survey Meter (FSM) was mounted on the table and was connected to the surface by cable running through a pipe, up to the ionisation chamber. The FSM, operated from within the underground post, could read up to 500 roentgens per hour increasing to more than 5000 roentgens per hour if the ionisation chamber was withdrawn down the pipe.

The Bomb Power Indicator (BPI) consisted of a baffle plate, mounted on a steel pipe on the surface. At the base of the pipe, in the monitoring room, an indicator unit with bellows was connected to a pointer. The over air pressure from the nuclear blast would pass down the pipe to the bellows, with the dial showing pressures of up to 5 pounds per square inch.

The third piece of instrumentation was the Ground Zero Indicator (GZI), which was quite simply a camera that had four pin-sized holes facing the cardinal compass points. A piece of photographic paper was placed in front of each hole and in the event of a nuclear blast, the image of a fireball would be projected onto the paper. From these, the bearings and evaluation of the blast could be calculated. Due to the GZI being mounted on top of the ventilation shaft next to the entrance hatch, this required somebody to emerge after the explosion to retrieve the sheets of paper!

All posts were issued with hand operated "Secomak" or "Carter" sirens, which would be used for sounding the "Red" warning (a rising and falling note) indicating an imminent air or missile attack and the "White" warning (a steady note), indicating the all clear. With the approach of radioactive fallout, the "Black" warning was sounded by maroons with a series of three explosions at close-set intervals.

Three Observers at work in an underground post. The Bomb Power Indicator (BPI) dial can be seen on the left along with the bunk bed and steel ventilation shutter in the background. (The Royal Observer Corps Historic Collection)

Most underground posts were also supplied with the following;
Torch
Pickaxe
Spade
Broom
Utensils
Cutlery
Kettle
Soap
Cooker and packets of fuel
Toilet paper – Hard government issue
Post Log – A diary of all exercises carried out in the post
Visitors log – Signed by all visitors to the post including BT engineers
Posters – Cloud, aircraft identification and first aid
Maps – Ordinance Survey maps and post cluster maps, generally laminated
Forms – Various
Photographic paper – For Ground Zero Indicator (GZI)
Siren box – Slatted wooden box approximately 24 x 15 x 15 inches
Dosimeters with charging unit – Purpose of use explained on page 38
Mirror with 12-volt strip light – Usually above shelf
Time switch – To ensure the light was never left on when the post was vacated
Fire blanket – In red metal box, generally located by the time switch
First Aid items – to be found in a bag or wooden box
Entrance shaft safety signage – To remind individuals of the 15ft drop
Enamel or plastic bucket
Waste bin
Rubber gloves
Baffle plates – For Bomb Power Indicator (BPI)
Gaskets – For Fixed Survey Meter probe (FSM)
BPI mounting board – Circular board to which the BPI is attached
Tool rack – Containing various tools, including an 18-inch crowbar
15-inch metal rod with two lugs – To remove the aerial connection point cover
Full body splint
Clock – Medium sized
Jerry cans – Containing water for drinking and general washing
Rope and cargo net – For hauling heavy objects up the entrance shaft
12-volt batteries
Steel sump grill – Covering sump at the bottom of the entrance shaft ladder
Sump pump handle – To pump any water in the sump to the surface through a
pipe fitted to the side of the entrance shaft

Side view of a Royal Observer Corps underground post.
(The National Archives)

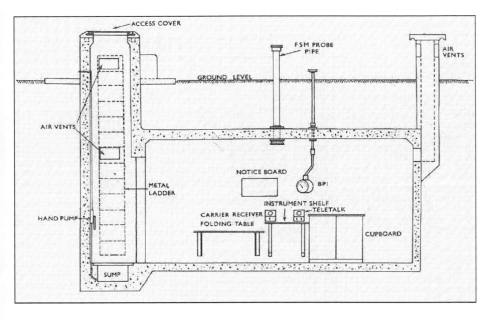

Aerial view of a Royal Observer Corps underground post.
(The National Archives)

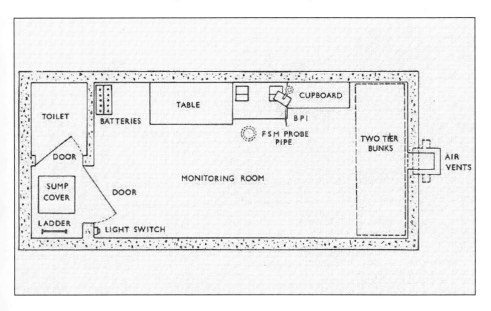

A Further image of a Royal Observer Corps underground post can be seen below, although in this instance, as a cutaway view. (Subterrranea Britannica)

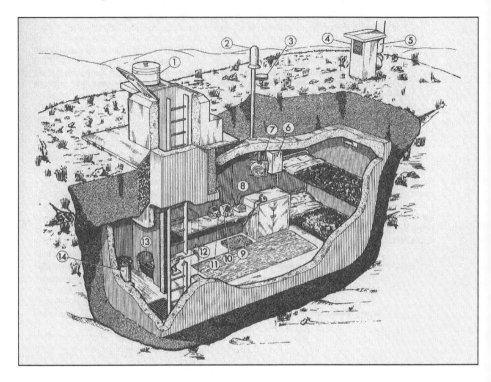

Key to numbers shown on image are as follows;

1) Ground zero indicator
2) Fixed survey meter probe cover
3) Bomb power indicator baffle plate
4) Air ventilator
5) Pneumatic antenna mast for radio set
6) Radio set
7) Bomb power indicator
8) Fixed survey meter
9) Radio head set
10) Loud speaker telephone
11) Carrier receiver
12) Pump for pneumatic antenna
13) 12 volt battery
14) Chemical toilet

Originally, underground posts were clustered into three's and four's for communication purposes. Group Headquarters would pass the information received from each post to Sector Operation Centres where scientists would forecast which areas would be in danger from nuclear fallout. In Lancing's case, the Royal Observer Corps volunteers would report to Group Headquarters in Horsham, West Sussex.

Communications between posts and Group Headquarters, such as Horsham, was by GPO telephone lines and in 1964 the conventional headset and microphone was replaced by "Tele-talk" an 8-inch square box containing a microphone and amplifier. In case of emergencies, all Group Headquarters and one post in each cluster were equipped with VHF radios and radio masts, these posts being known as master posts.

In the summer of 1965, the last remaining surface posts were closed down as the Royal Air Force decided that it no longer required the Royal Observer Corps in the aircraft recognition and reporting role. Due to the speed of these fighter planes, the reporting system was now inadequate. Radar had advanced greatly and with the development of airborne early warning aircraft such as the Shackleton, Nimrod and AWACS, this had overcome other radar problems, in finding aircraft hidden from ground-based radar by hills, buildings, etc.

The Royal Observer Corps would remain a uniformed organisation under the control of the Royal Air Force, however would continue with the nuclear monitoring role, still being required to report to the United Kingdom Warning Monitoring Organisation (UKWMO).

One Sunday morning in the mid 1960's (date unknown), an open day was held at the Lancing underground post to give members of the public some idea of what the Royal Observer Corps were doing on their doorstep. It was also hoped that by doing this, the Corps might obtain more volunteers. The Worthing Herald published a generously sized article on the Friday before explaining in detail the forth-coming open day. Three Photographs also appeared.

Titled "Observer Corps Post's Open Day", the Worthing Herald explained; "Beneath a one time refuse tip, within range of the public's gaze but seldom attracting it, is a Royal Observer Corps post. Directing operations from this skilfully concealed base to the north west of Brooklands boating pool, Chief Observer Horace Griffin – better known, perhaps, in his capacity as a Lancing postman – is confident of what his outfit could achieve in time of emergency.

But he is somewhat concerned that "the average man and woman in the street appear to know so little of our purpose and duties – if, indeed, they know of our existence at all."

In an effort to change all this Mr Griffin and the rest of his crew are holding an open day on Sunday. "We shall be ready to receive anyone interested from 10 in the morning until about sunset," he told the Herald, "but please make it clear that we are sorry but we just can't show children over the post."

The public will be able to examine some £1,000 worth of delicate equipment in the base – which measures 14ft by 10ft and questions will be welcome. What is the purpose of the post? The short answer is to detect and report enemy aerial activity and to register the extent of bomb blast and radiation.

Small projections of masonry above the ground beside Brooklands are the only signs marking the location of the Observer Corps Post.
(The Worthing Herald and Gazette / Portsmouth Publishing and Printing Ltd)

Mr H. Griffin removes the housing from a "ground zero" instrument situated above the post at Brooklands.
(The Worthing Herald and Gazette / Portsmouth Publishing and Printing Ltd)

Royal Observer Corps members Mr G. Taylor (seated) and
Mr A. W. Capel prepare for an exercise on monitoring an
imaginary nuclear bomb burst over the Worthing area.
(The Worthing Herald and Gazette / Portsmouth Publishing and Printing Ltd)

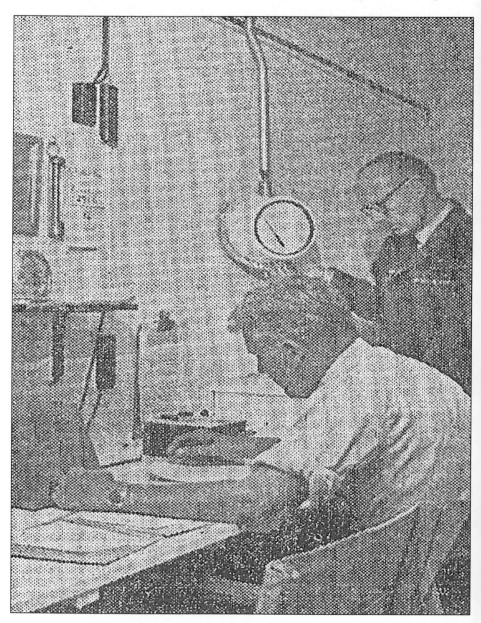

The Herald continued to report; "For practice exercises, details of simulated enemy attacks are prepared at Ministry level by "backroom" boys whose job it is to study local conditions, such as prevailing winds, and then pass them onto group headquarters at Horsham for redistribution to regional posts. By this means posts are able to gain experience in registering effects of the latest missiles exploded, while a small section of mica, cut into various widths, simulates shock waves (authors notes – instead of shock waves, the Herald should have put radiation / fallout levels) resulting from possible bomb attacks.

Post members meet at the Adult Education Centre every Friday; corps exercises are carried out about eight times a year. Membership, which at one time was as high as 24, is now down to 14. "We are appealing for more volunteers, both men and women," said Mr Griffin, "and anyone, between the ages of 16 to 60, is eligible for membership."

The post's second in command, Leading Observer Frederick Knight, is a laboratory technician at Beechams, Mr Geoff Taylor is a Post Office overseer, Mr Stan Green is a self-employed landscape gardener, Mr David Cossey is a Rustington postman and Mr Keith Butcher is a bank clerk.

The post's only woman observer is Miss Peggy Jones, a post office telephonist. Mr Taylor said the post was the only one sited in an old rubbish dump. This probably made it the best insulated post in the country. Its temperature on Saturday was 79 degrees Fahrenheit."

In January 1968, the Labour Government had decided that the threat of a nuclear attack had lessened. As part of huge reductions in defence spending many Home Office services were being abolished or curtailed. The future of the Royal Observer Corps looked uncertain.

On the 18th January 1968, a Home Office minister, made the following statement in the House of Commons; "The Royal Observer Corps will be retained as part of the United Kingdom Warning and Monitoring Organisation. It has the task of warning the public of an imminent attack with nuclear weapons and subsequently to warn them of nuclear fall-out. The organisation also has the ability to provide more detailed information, particularly on fall-out, to services, which can make use of it. Therefore we are making an exception to the general principle of winding up volunteer organisations although there will be some re-organisation and reduction to secure economies."

Throughout the country, the strength of the Corps was reduced from 25,000 to 12,500. This resulted in the closure of more than half the underground posts. Due to this personnel were asked to either leave the Corps, or move to the nearest surviving post.

Lancing was one of these posts chosen for closure and once a majority of the equipment had been taken out by contractors, the hatch was closed and locked for good in October 1968. Several of the Lancing personnel moved to the Steyning Post, whereas several others who came from the west of the area went to the Littlehampton Post (actually on Ford Aerodrome).

The post at Lancing may have closed, however it would appear as though the Ministry of Defence continued to lease the land and maintain the post until the end of 1970. Minutes for a Worthing Borough Council meeting held on 13th November 1970 explained;

"Brooklands Pleasure Park-Royal Observer Post. The town Clerk reported that the Ministry of Defence had given notice to terminate their lease of the land at Brooklands on which they had constructed an Observer Post. RESOLVED, that notice be accepted, subject to the Ministry of Defence re-instating the land in accordance with the terms of the lease."

The post's surface features were demolished shortly after and the land was returned to how it once was. The cost of demolishing and filling in such an underground post would have been a costly procedure and so it is very likely that the bunker remains intact below the surface.

Once the surface features were demolished, the holes to the entrance shaft, ventilation shafts, Fixed Survey Meter pipe and the Bomb Power Indicator pipe were probably covered using thick slabs of concrete, which were then levelled with earth and then finally turfed over to blend in with the remaining area. It is also possible to assume that some furniture may still remain in the post. For example, the bunk beds were generally not removed from posts closed in 1968, but they were generally removed from posts closed in 1991.

Prior to the 1968 reorganisation there were no limits to the number of observers within a post, however after the 1968 reorganisation, each post was limited to a maximum of just ten. This figure would comprise of a head or chief observer, leading observer who was also the post instructor and eight ordinary observers.

This allowed for three shifts, although in reality this number was often difficult to achieve and it was quite common for neighbouring posts to stand in when required. The three observers on duty at any one time were numbered one, two and three.

Number one observer was in charge of the post and was responsible for reading and accessing the information from the Ground Zero Instrument (GZI) and Bomb Power Indicator (BPI). Number two observer was in charge of communications, checking the GZI and BPI readings, reading the Fixed Survey Meter (FSM), filling in the post log and reporting the readings to Group Headquarters. Number three observer was responsible for the GZI and the domestic side of the post.

National exercises (WARMON) were held, usually twice a year and would usually take place on a Sunday for a duration of 8 hours. International exercises (INTEX) would also take place once a year and would link up with other warning and monitoring organisations throughout Europe.

There was also one or two Corps exercises a year, which generally consisted of a re-run of a previous WARMON or INTEX exercises. Cluster meetings would take place once every three months where all the observers from each cluster would get together and individual post meetings were usually held once a week to test the equipment, phone lines etc and for training purposes.

It was agreed by the Home Office and the Ministry of Defence that the Royal Observer Corps would cease active training at the end of July 1991 and would stand down in its operational role at the end of September, full time staff continuing the run down until 31st March 1992. The United Kingdom Warning Monitoring Organisation (UKWMO) would also stand down.

During my research I was extremely fortunate to speak with several ex Royal Observer Corps Lancing Post volunteers, although sadly searches for Observers in service before this time proved unsuccessful.

Eric Bunce recalls his half brother, Harry Thomas Bunce, was an Observer on the end of Worthing Pier and then moved to the roof of the County Restaurant in Marine Parade when the pier was blown/sectioned. Harry, Managing Director of the family business (Bunce's Home Hardware), was Head Observer and received an OBE for his services, along with a photograph of all wartime Observers. Today, the whereabouts of this photograph is unclear.

Moving on to the Cold war era, Fred Knight, Horace Griffin, Keith Butcher and Paul Wakefield all recall their years in the Royal Observer Corps. All had an interest in aircraft recognition and it is mainly due to this that they joined the Corps. It is interesting to note that all have questioned how long the crew in an underground post would have survived following a nuclear attack and whether members of the ROC would actually have turned up for duty. All agree that thankfully their role was never put to the test.

Keith Butcher recalls; " I enrolled in 1963 because I had an interest in aircraft recognition. I remember the Lancing Post well. People would often come up to the post at Lancing, believing it was a reservoir and would ask what we were doing with the town's water supply. Being located in a pleasure park, kids would also come up to the post and ask what we were doing.

The fun fair would visit now and again and was placed on the higher ground next to our post. It was not unusual to have swinging chairs flying through the air over our post. When Lancing Post closed, I moved to Steyning Post until 1973 and then went on to Littlehampton Post. In 1979 I moved to 36 Hambledon Post in Hampshire and stayed there until the Royal Observer Corps was stood down."

Following a conversation with Paul Wakefield, he kindly spent valuable time to write down his thoughts on his years in the Royal Observer Corps. He explains; "I was enrolled in the Royal Observer Corps on the 23rd October 1964, as a member of the Worthing Post, designated 2/E.2. An existing member, Claude Porter, had made me aware of its existence for the first time, when I worked for a builder's merchants in Dominion Road, and the building company that Claude worked for, shared the same yard.

He bought materials from us, so I saw a lot of him. He was very interested in aircraft, and would often point them out to me when they flew over. When I told him I was keen to learn how to identify them, he suggested that I visited his house on a Sunday morning, where he would teach me.

His house, in Oakleigh Road, was on the edge of Worthing, and only had allotments to the east of it, so, from his conservatory, we could see aircraft taking off from Shoreham Airport, and also those flying down the outbound airway which passed overhead. He taught me how to recognise and name them, and also told me about the ROC, and how they reported their movements. I was eventually so interested, that I wanted to join.

I can recall my mother's horror, when I told her of my intentions, as she assumed that I was joining the army for 20 years. Post meetings were held each Friday evening, at a room in the Drill Hall, Forest Road, (which is now the Freemason's Lodge), in a small room with seats all around, and hundreds of model aircraft hanging from the darkened ceiling. In the centre of the room was a huge epidiascope, which was a device used to project photographs of aircraft onto a screen, so that we could identify them.

There were two NCO's on the post, Chief Observer Peter Wadey, who was head of the Worthing Post and dealt with the administration, and Leading Observer Horace Griffin, ("Griff"), who was responsible for training.
I had only been a member of "Echo Two" for a couple of years, when sadly, Peter Wadey, the Chief Observer was killed in a road accident. The post members, including myself, provided a Guard of Honour at his funeral at Angmering Parish Church. After this, Griff took over as Chief, and a new Leading Observer was appointed.

Normal membership of each post was intended to be about 10 – 12 observers, but this number varied from time to time, sometimes as many as 15/20, or as few as 6/7.

Members came from all walks of life, and those I recall, as well as the two NCO's were: Ian Croad, an architect from Lancing, who eventually went on to become an Observer Officer, (responsible for several posts), Dave Cossey, a postman from Rustington, Stan Green, a landscape gardener from Rustington, Keith Butcher, a bank clerk, Barry Somerville, Fred Knight, a laboratory technician at Beechams. He was on the Henfield post with his father, but transferred to Worthing when he came to work and live in the town. Geoff Taylor, who worked at the GPO, Arthur Capel, (civil servant) and at one time, Peggy Jones, a telephonist, who was our first woman observer.

We were all issued with a uniform, which consisted of an RAF blue' grey jacket and trousers, blue shirt, with a black tie and a black beret with an ROC cap badge. The jackets had markings on each shoulder; to identify which Group the observer belonged to.

On each arm could be a 'Spitfire' insignia, which indicated the observer's level of proficiency, which had been proved by an annual exam called "The Master Test." If a mark of 90% or more had been achieved, the observer was allowed to display a blue spitfire on his arm.

When he had done this at least 5 times, the spitfire was changed to red. After 10, I think a red star was added, and so on. The annual Master Test exam was usually held on a Sunday morning, and took place at various venues over the years. I recall going to the barn theatre at Field Place one year, and then later on it was regularly held in the restaurant at the Excess Insurance Company in Hillbarn Lane. Before I joined, when part of the exam included an aircraft recognition test film, the venue was the Odeon cinema in Worthing.

A monthly magazine, "The Royal Observer Corps Journal" was published, and each observer received a copy. The journal gave all kinds of news of members, promotions, etc, and also gave lessons in aircraft recognition, and aspects of nuclear reporting. Also in the journal was a regular aircraft recognition competition called "Airborne Headaches", and each post was invited to submit their answers for the reward of an annual presentation cup. One of our members, Keith Butcher, was, and still is, an expert in aircraft recognition, and E2 always did very well in the competition, largely thanks to him.

The local posts were supervised in 'clusters' of 3 or 4 posts, by a part-time Observer Officer, who would visit each post on a regular basis. There were two other posts in our cluster, at Littlehampton, (Ford Aerodrome) and Pulborough.

When I enrolled, our Officer was a chap called Fisher, but within a few months he was succeeded by Jack Fannon, who had moved to Worthing as a Public Health Inspector for Worthing Borough Council. Jack stayed with us for many years, and we got to know him and his wife very well. One of his very first duties was the organisation of the Guard of Honour for our Chief Observer's funeral.

In addition to local meetings, we also had regular "Cluster Meetings", which were an opportunity to meet members from the other two posts in our cluster, and occasionally two clusters. These meetings were sometimes held at the public house in Lancing called The Britannia, (now the Harvester), sometimes at Arundel or Pulborough.

There were also two annual Group Meetings, when all the posts in the Group could meet up with the members at Headquarters. One of them was a fairly formal 'do', rather like an AGM, and took place at Horsham, but the other annual group meeting was much more interesting. This took place at Thorney Island near the Sussex/Hampshire border and was our nearest RAF Transport Command station.

There, after a brief administration session, we were split up into parties, which then proceeded to have a tour of the complete base, the hangars, the control tower, the flight simulators, and the fire station.

I can even recall that a special flying display by a Hawker Hunter was arranged. The highlight of the day, however, was an air experience flight. On my first visits to Thorney, the flights were in a Blackburn Beverley, which usually trundled around the Isle of Wight, but later, the aircraft were updated to A.W. Argosys and H.S. Andovers. One lucky group had the good fortune to fly to the Channel Islands in an Argosy, where they made a 'touch and go' at Jersey airport.

When the ROC was first formed, its role was to identify and report aircraft movements, and it performed this role with great distinction during World War Two. With the development of radar, however, and the increasing speed of aircraft making reporting difficult, it was decided to phase out this particular duty during the 1960's, and find a new job for the Corps.

During the so called "Cold War", the government had to consider the real possibility of a nuclear attack on this country, and there was a requirement for some sort of confirmation that an attack had taken place, followed by an appreciation of the likely path and intensity of any resultant fall-out and radiation. This job was given to the ROC, with the resultant development of the underground monitoring post.

It must be remembered, however, that, the majority of observer corps members had a great interest in aircraft, and it may have been that most of them had joined for that reason, and so, to suddenly drop the aircraft aspect from the Corps' role would have resulted in mass resignation of personnel.

When I joined in 1964, we were still involved in both aircraft reporting and nuclear monitoring. In addition to the weekly meetings at the drill hall, we also held exercises at our underground post site at Brooklands, on the Worthing - Lancing boundary.

The actual site was on land to the west of the paddling pool adjacent to the boating lake, which had been built up when the area was part of the refuse tip operated by the local authority. This meant that the post was actually built into the decaying refuse, and as a result of the decay, the temperature inside the underground post was constantly in the high 70's, winter or summer.

This made it a very comfortable environment in which to operate, and we were the envy of the surrounding posts, most of which were damp and cold. The post consisted of a large reinforced concrete room, buried about 2 metres below ground. It was reached by a small concrete shaft just large enough to accommodate a fairly well built observer, with a vertical ladder down to the monitoring room, which was separated from the shaft by a door.

The shaft also had another small room from it, which acted as a toilet, but also, inevitably a storage facility. The access shaft contained louvers for ventilation, and a sump at the base, covered by a grating, with a hand operated pump, in case of any flooding within the post. The shaft projected about a metre above ground, and was sealed by a 600x 600mm manhole cover on top, which was hinged and counterbalanced, so that it could be locked in the open position. It could also be locked shut by a large turnkey, and was secured later by the addition of two large padlocks.

Getting in and out of the post could be a precarious procedure, as contained within the shaft was a large counterbalance weight, which gave you a nasty headache if you banged your head on it going up, and a large vertical wooden handle of a sump pump, which could do indescribable damage when going down! The latter was deemed to be so dangerous, that it was later reversed to point sideways, which made it more awkward if it had to be used for pumping.

Above ground all that was visible of the post was the access shaft with the cover, a ventilation shaft with louvers at the other end of the post, and various pipes, covers and stands stood ready to receive the various instruments we used to carry out our duties. A large net on the end of a rope was provided, and this was used to haul items of equipment and tools up and down the shaft, for use above ground.

Inside the room, which was approx. 5 metres x 2 metres, was a two-tier bunk, a storage cupboard, a table fixed to the wall, and chairs for the crew of three. There was another air vent at the opposite end to the shaft, and a set of 12-volt batteries to supply lighting.

The batteries had to be charged regularly by means of a small petrol-electric generator above ground, with leads to the batteries, and connection of them had to be very precise, as any reverse of polarity would have caused great damage. It was also very important to keep the post ventilators and hatch open, so that any gas from the charging batteries was dispersed safely.

There was no running water, so the toilet provided, was an 'Elsan' type, which had to be charged with special fluid before use, and hauled up the shaft when it had to be emptied, so invariably it was not used more than absolutely necessary during exercises, because of the effort required in emptying it.

Drinking water was stored in 25 litre jerry cans, and these had to be replenished regularly, so hauling them up and down the shaft on a rope was also quite an effort. Although official WD food ration packs were provided, they were intended for use only in an emergency, and during time spent in the post, we were expected to bring our own food supplies from home.

The only time we were allowed to use the rations were when the shelf-life date expired, and they had to be disposed of. Some of the food was very interesting. The ration pack included a small methylated spirit heater, for warming up some of the food, but, obvious safety precautions had to be taken within our confined area, and cooking had to be done at the foot of the shaft.

To communicate with our Group Headquarters, which was at Horsham, a telephone line was run to the post. When I first joined, the observer using it wore a 'head and breast set', similar to those used by post office telephonists, which was basically a pair of headphones with a mouthpiece attached. Only the person using them could hear the talk on the line, but after a while, they were replaced by a 'Teletalk', a small metal box with a loudspeaker facing the user.

A switch on the front converted the speaker to a microphone, so that the operator, and all the observers in the posts could hear any incoming messages, and then, by depressing the switch, a message could be sent back to Horsham Control. The lines were arranged, so that the other two posts within our cluster could also be overheard.

Sometimes, when the lines failed, we found that we could talk to the other two posts, but not the Control. Occasionally, two clusters could be connected to the same circuit, so maybe 6 or 7 posts could be overheard.

In addition to the Teletalk, there was a similar looking device called a 'Carrier Warning Receiver', but the communication was only one-way. It had to be switched on at the start of any time spent in the post, and remain on all the time. To indicate it was working, it emitted a constant re-assuring 'pip tone, rather similar to the GMT pips on the radio, but, thankfully, the volume could be adjusted so that it didn't drive us up the wall!

These receivers were also installed in all centres of administration, such as Police Stations, Local Government offices, and utility establishments, and they would be, in the case of emergencies, our means of receiving warnings of imminent nuclear attacks, and also danger of radiation from fall-out.

Warning of a nuclear attack (the so-called four minute warning) was provided by an eerie wailing noise, but other verbal warnings of fall out were actually issued at a local level by the Police, and, strangely, based on information provided by our post monitoring in the first place.

The Carrier Receiver was routinely tested, which usually meant a special visit to the post to hear it, and it was quite a strange feeling to hear it working. All the time the regular tone, like a heart beat, was heard, it gave us a comforting feeling that 'all was right in the world', but when that was suddenly replaced by a different sound, it was a frightening thought of what would be happening outside if ever the sounds were heard for real.

Part of our role was to warn the public in the surrounding area, and to do this, we had a small hand-operated siren, which we had to turn at full speed for 5 seconds, then let it run down for the same time, and keep repeating this procedure for a full minute, thus producing the familiar siren rising and falling sound associated with World War 2. We also had maroons, which were fired electronically, and this was the warning of imminent fall-out danger. The public were not generally made aware of this warning, but I'm sure would have been, should a crisis have arisen.

We had various instruments to carry out our monitoring duties. Fixed to the wall above the desk in the monitoring room was the Bomb Power Indicator, or BPI, which consisted of a large round dial, with a needle, which registered air pressure from zero to 5 lbs per square inch. The dial was connected vertically, by a steel pipe, to a horizontal baffle, made up of two 150mm round steel plates, about 10mm apart, which projected just above ground level.

If a nuclear explosion had occurred within our range, it would have produced a pressure wave, which, as it passed over the post, would have entered the baffle, and caused a reading to show on the dial inside the post. This would have been the first indication that a bomb had been detonated locally, and reporting of any reading was regarded as top priority. A message to Control with a reading was prefixed by a priority code 'Tocsin', followed by our post designation, and the pressure reading.

Another instrument was called the Ground Zero Indicator, or GZI, and this was fixed to a purpose made bracket, usually attached to the post access shaft. This was basically a set of four pinhole cameras, each one facing the cardinal points of the compass, north, south, east and west. Four sheets of very low light sensitive paper were enclosed within a transparent celluloid envelope, upon which were marked the compass point, and a grid which divided the paper up into degrees of horizontal bearings, and vertical elevations.

The envelope and paper were then installed into the camera, and a large round cover was screw fixed over the whole assembly. The sensitivity of the paper was such that it could remain inside the camera without darkening for several days. Light subjects, such as the sun, would burn a trail onto the paper, as did any other bright objects within range.

The Ground Zero Instrument was screwed to a purpose made bracket, which was set in the concrete of the hatch cover top, and it could only be fitted facing one way, thus ensuring the orientation towards the points of the compass was always accurate. In the event of a nuclear explosion, the flash from the bomb would burn a spot onto the paper, and from this spot, the bearing of the bomb from our post, the elevation in the sky, and the size of the spot could be measured and reported.

At Horsham headquarters, our information, plus similar reports from other local posts could all be plotted, by a triangulation team, on a map, and from the data, they could tell, from cross-bearings, exactly where the bombs had dropped, from elevations, whether they were 'ground' or 'air' bursts, (which would determine how much, if any fallout would be produced).

In addition, by using the size of the spot and the first pressure reading that we had reported, they could also estimate the size of the bomb dropped. This information was then combined with meteorological forecasts, so that a projected path of likely fallout, its likely intensity could be estimated, and necessary warnings issued to the public to take cover.

Our other main instrument was called a Fixed Survey Meter, (FSM), and this measured the rate at which radiation was occurring outside our post. In the ceiling of the post, was a circular opening, approximately 120mm diameter, this being the lower end of a large steel pipe with a flange on it. The upper end of the pipe projected about 900mm above ground, onto which was bolted a large heavy-duty plastic cover, with a domed top.

The radiation sensor part of the FSM was fixed to the top of a telescopic rod, which was the right dimensions to be inserted into the round tube in the ceiling, and when fully extended up the tube, the sensor would be at the uppermost part of the plastic dome cover.

A cable from the sensor, led back down the tube, and was connected to a meter, which sat on the monitoring room table. When radiation first appeared outside the post, the meter would register, and this reading was reported. This information would serve to confirm the assessment team's initial forecast, or prediction, and correct and amend any public warnings. After the first reading, subsequent readings were reported every five minutes, and in this way, a map of radiation intensity all over the country could be made.

In addition to all those instruments, each observer was issued with his own personal dosimeter, which registered how much radiation he had received. Limits as to how much radiation could be safely absorbed were always in force, so that, using this information, any requirement for an observer to carry out any duty above ground, e.g. changing the papers in the GZI, would be made by the one who had received the lowest dose.

As well as providing information from within the post, there was an additional scheme, called Mobile Monitoring, where members of the post crew would, if circumstances permitted, venture outside the post to report on conditions in the locality, such as the state of bridges, roads, railways, etc, information which might be vital when considering evacuation of the population.

Such expeditions would only have been undertaken if levels of radiation were such that they posed a limited threat to the personnel who carried them out. During peacetime exercises, it was obviously impossible to carry out realistic training, so alternatives were developed. For reporting bomb pressures, we were just given a figure to report at a certain time, but pre-prepared mock papers for the GZI were produced, and these had to be assessed by us, and then the bearing, elevation, spot size, etc were reported.

A clever version of the Fixed Survey meter was also invented, and this consisted of a clockwork-operated motor, which pulled a celluloid strip past the lower end of the needle on the dial. By pre-cutting the strip into a variable predetermined shape, this made the needle on the dial register rise and fall, simulating a radiation level outside the post. These readings were then reported as normal.

Due to the limited ventilation in the post, restrictions on the time that the post could be 'closed' were always in place during exercises. It had been calculated that a normal crew would use up the available air in approximately 7 hours, so each post was forbidden to be closed for any longer than that. The state of each post in the group was strictly monitored at Control, to ensure that this rule was never broken. Devices to mechanically ventilate some posts were experimented with, but not at Lancing.

As well as the annual written 'Master Test' exam, which tested us on our theory knowledge, the Corps also developed a practical test, which took the form of an annual competition between posts in the Group. Having selected a crew of three to represent our post (usually done by the short straw method), a senior Observer Officer would visit the post under operational conditions, and he would see how we set up and operated all our equipment, and how we monitored and reported our data, and mark us accordingly. There was also a trophy awarded to the post adjudged to be the most proficient.

As mentioned previously, the role of reporting aircraft was still undertaken, and similar above ground exercises took place. The task was to locate any aircraft within visible range of the post, identify its type (if possible), and then estimate its altitude, bearing from the post, and its direction of travel. All this information would be reported to the Group Control.

To assist us in the estimation of a bearing, we had a circular plotting table on a tripod, marked with 360 degrees, plus obvious visible landmarks, such as church steeples, and by aligning the landmark with a mark on the table ensured that it was also aligned with due north. Sometimes, when conditions were cloudy, or, at night time, when the aircraft couldn't be seen, then a 'sound only' report was given.

Very high aircraft could often not be seen, but the resulting condensation trail from their engines, or 'contrail', was visible, so it was reported as such. We were usually given 'the contrail height' from the met office, which helped us to estimate the altitude of such aircraft. I can recall a couple of occasions when the RAF actually flew aircraft around the area, say, for an evening exercise, so that we could practice our identification and reporting skills.

In 1968, the Government of the time decided that the threat of a possible nuclear war was receding, and, in an effort to save money, as often happens, it was decided that the size of the ROC should be reduced.

In practical terms, this meant that, roughly, every other post was closed down, and the personnel were asked to either leave the Corps, or move to the nearest surviving post. I, with several others, opted to move to the Steyning post, whereas several others who came from the west of our area went to the Littlehampton Post (actually on Ford Aerodrome).

At the time, it was sad to break up our happy team, but we soon melded in with our new surroundings, and we continued until the Corps was stood down completely in 1991."

Ex Lancing Post members can be seen above in this photograph showing the Observers at 46 Steyning Post 2/J2 circa 1975. Back row left to right are; Claude Porter, Fred Osborne, Horace Griffin (Griff), Fred Knight and Paul Wakefield. Front row left to right are; Mervyn King, Harry Dearlove, Chief Observer Paul Norris and Leading Observer Ernie Woodbridge. (Paul Wakefield)

Paul Wakefield is seen below in the compound of 46 Steyning Post 2/J2.
(Paul Wakefield)

Paul Wakefield is seen below, standing in the vicinity of the Lancing underground post in August 2007. The boating lake can be seen in the background. (Authors Collection)

Paul Wakefield continued to explain; "As members of the post, we often discussed the potential effectiveness of the Royal Observer Corps, should the need have arisen to use our skills for real. In the time of a real emergency, we would have been expected to attend for duty, leaving our family and loved ones at home to fend for themselves. We even worked out a plan for our families to get together to help each other.

Whether or not, in reality, some, or all of the members would actually have turned up for duty, thankfully was never put to the test. Personally, I doubt it. I have also often considered how long the crew in an underground post would have survived following a nuclear attack, and I think the answer would be 'probably not very long'.

Long enough, however, to have carried out the primary objective required of the Corps, i.e. to confirm the attack and the extent of it, and then anything after that would have been a bonus, subject to the crew's survival. In any case, their life expectancy would hopefully have been longer than anyone left above ground under horrendous circumstances, which don't bear thinking about, and thankfully was never put to the test."

Having almost completed this publication I had become very keen to visit an underground Royal Observer Corps Post. I was deeply disappointed when I learnt that the Lancing Post was no more. I wished it was possible to liase with Worthing Borough Council to uncover the Lancing Post and gain entry, although knew that this would not be possible.

To appreciate what life was like within one of these underground posts, I decided to arrange a visit to one, which had survived such punishment. A visit to many of the local underground posts proved unsuccessful, however excitement struck when I was able to arrange a visit with the landowners of a post extremely local to Lancing Post. Due to the landowner's wishes, the location of this post, sadly, cannot be disclosed.

Arrangements were made with all parties concerned and the visit took place on Sunday 20th January 2008 at 2pm. Present were ex Royal Observer Corps Steyning Post members Paul Wakefield and Paul Norris and the landowners (who wish to remain nameless) and I. Our vehicles were parked on a tarmac access road, which had been laid by the government purposely for Royal Observer Corps personnel to gain access to the field in which the bunker was sited.

The surface features of the underground post were visible and as we neared these it soon became apparent that the landowners had no idea what the bunker had been used for or even who had used it. They would soon be given a constructive history lesson.

Armed with a camera, the entrance hatch was unlocked using the original key and once lifted, we took it in turn to climb down the extremely narrow 15 ft shaft. As explained previously the post was originally powered by a 12-volt battery, but for our visit, we had to make do with several torches and a lantern.

Once inside, it was quite an experience watching the emotions of the ex Royal Observer Corps members on their visit, being confined once again to one of these posts. We found original paperwork and surprisingly much equipment had survived – mattresses from the bunks, government supply toilet paper, even the toilet itself. The power and communication cables, switches, table, chairs, shelf and cabinet were still present.

Paul Wakefield can be seen, climbing into the entrance shaft while one of the landowners looks on. Other surface features include the ventilation shaft on the right, the Fixed Survey Meter pipe in the middle and the Bomb Power Indicator pipe also in the middle of this photograph, although out of site within the grass.
(Authors Collection)

The Fixed Survey Meter pipe (top left) and the Bomb Power Indicator pipe (bottom right). These pipes retain the covers, which were always screwed in place when the attached instrumentation was dismantled. (Authors Collection)

Paul Norris begins his descent of the entrance shaft. (Authors Collection)

A view of the entrance hatch, locks, ladder and entrance shaft.
(Authors Collection)

A photograph showing the first room, still containing
the chemical toilet and tools. (Authors Collection)

The monitoring room. The ventilation shaft shutter can be seen at the rear, mattresses still wrapped in their polythene, jerry cans, table and cabinet. The hole for the Fixed Survey Meter probe to be inserted into the FSM pipe can be seen on the roof (top left). The Bomb Power Indicator and wooden board in which the Bomb Power Indicator dial was attached can also be seen on the left. (Authors Collection)

A closer view of the Bomb Power Indicator and wooden board in which the Bomb Power Indicator dial was attached. Note the polystyrene tiles which were added to all underground posts to give them some sort of insulation. Electric cable for the single 12-volt light bulb (out of view) can also be seen. (Authors Collection)

This views shows where the 12-volt batteries were once placed. One can see the power cable still exists, complete with battery connectors crimped onto the ends of the wires. With the power cable in excellent condition and the single light bulb still in place and undamaged, one wonders if the power could be quite simply reinstated on a following visit. An original enamel bucket with lid can also be seen. (Authors Collection)

The cabinet, which contained various items, including government supply toilet paper. One interesting feature was the 1991 Royal Navy calendar seen here on the table, which incidentally displayed September – the year this particular post closed when the Corps stood down in September 1991. (Authors Collection)

Paul Wakefield is seen here using the monitoring room door keys from Brighton underground post. It was suggested that they might work here, although it soon became apparent that a different lock had been used. Other features in this photograph include the light switch timer on the left of the door frame (to ensure the light was never left on when the post was vacated), fixing holes on the left (where the fire blanket container was fitted) and a clock, located on the top shelf. After winding this up, we were staggered to learn that it still worked. (Authors Collection)

We remained in the post for almost 45 minutes talking about the role of the Corps and in particular the effectiveness of the post if the country had have been attacked with a nuclear warhead.

Once our visit had been documented and photographed, we climbed back up to the surface, avoiding hitting our head on the hatch counterweight, closed the hatch and locked the post. Our appreciation was given to the landowners for a very enjoyable visit.

Overview

Despite the role the Royal Observer Corps had played, it completely baffles me as to why they were not better known. It appears as though they should have been given much more credit than they were actually given. For the individuals involved, working in all weathers and then later being moved to a small underground bunker, lit by a single 12 volt bulb must have been severely uninviting.

Today, the landmarks in which the original two roof posts were located can be visited. However access onto the roof of the south pavilion of Worthing Pier and The County Restaurant in Marine Parade, now known as The Connaught Corner House Restaurant, is obviously denied. The site of the underground post built at Brooklands Pleasure Park can also be visited, although as previously explained, sadly no surface features remain.

I believe that there is much more to learn about the Royal Observer Corps in Worthing during the Second World War, however I do feel that the corps's role in Worthing during the Cold War is now well documented in this publication. My research on the Royal Observer Corps has been a worthwhile and enjoyable journey. Like all other past projects it has, on some occasions been very difficult to piece it all together.

I have met some very interesting and helpful individuals along the way and if it had not been for these, this publication would not have been possible to compile.

I welcome any comments or additions that may be able to further this subject.

Graham Lelliott

Further Information

Those who wish to learn more about the Royal Observer Corps in general may find the following of some interest;

"Attack Warning Red" by Derek Wood, published by Carmichael and Sweet of Portsmouth. It is an incredible piece of work, which gives a detailed account of the Royal Observer Corps and the defence of Britain from 1925 to 1992.

Subterranea Britannica, a group within the United Kingdom, who record all underground manmade and man used places. The group has a fantastic website, which includes much information and photographs of many underground sites throughout the country. It has, in particular, a section devoted to the Royal Observer Corps, which gives information on all 1,563 underground posts.

The Royal Observer Corps Historic Collection can be seen at Newhaven Fort in Newhaven, East Sussex. As explained in the introduction, it is due to this fine exhibition, which inspired this publication. Well worth a visit.

At this time, The Royal Observer Corps Museum's collection is housed in leased premises in Winchester, Hampshire, although they do have a small exhibition within Solent Sky in Southampton (previously Southampton Hall of Aviation). The museums Royal Observer Corps archives can be viewed upon request at Hampshire County Record Office in Winchester.

Many Royal Observer Corps Orlit and underground posts survive to this day, some however have fallen into disrepair or have been vandalised. If you intend to explore any of these sites do not trespass on any private property or cause damage to property whilst attempting to explore. Seek permission from the landowner first and ensure you take proper and sensible precautions regarding your personal safety. It is essential you explore with at least one other person, especially at underground sites.

Only a handful of the underground posts have been purchased and restored to their former glory. The following open to the public on certain days in the year; Veryan in Cornwall, Ashwell in Hertfordshire, Knockholt in Kent, Rushton Spencer in Staffordshire, Wroughton in Wiltshire and Skelmorlie, Ayrshire.

Many Royal Observer Corps sites can be found on the Internet, including The Royal Observer Corps Association.

Acknowledgements

My sincere thanks go to the following people, organisations and sources;

Tim Yates
Mike Franklin
Paul Wakefield
Horace Griffin
Fred Knight
Keith Butcher
Paul Norris
Ian Burrows
Jenny Morris
Alan Redman
Nick Catford
Greg Smith
Jane Dore
Freddie Feest
Martin Hayes
Tony Maasz
Neville Cullingford
Graeme Finlayson
Frank Alexander
Katherine McGlinchey
Kate Loubser
Cliff Harrison
Yvonne Ferguson
Mark Stephen
Eric Bunce
Martin Mace
Hampshire County Council, Winchester, Hampshire
Hampshire County Records Office, Winchester, Hampshire
The Royal Observer Corps Trust
The Royal Observer Corps Association
The Royal Observer Corps Historic Collection
The Royal Observer Corps Museum
Subterranea Britannica
Worthing Library
Worthing Borough Council
Worthing Herald and Gazette

Worthing Museum and Art Gallery
Tangmere Military Aviation Museum, Chichester, West Sussex.
The Imperial War Museum, London
The Home Office, London
The Worthing Argus
The Worthing Sentinel
Portsmouth Publishing and Printing Ltd, West Sussex Division
The West Sussex Gazette
The National Archives, Kew, Surrey
Imperial War Museum, London
Newhaven Fort, Newhaven, East Sussex
The West Sussex Records Office, Chichester, West Sussex
MOD Air Historical Branch, RAF Bentley Priory, Stanmore, Middlesex
Crown Copyright / Ministry of Defence, London

I would also like to thank the following, who kindly published my Worthing
Royal Observer Corps enquiries in order to help me further this project;

Britain at War Magazine.
Article published in April 2008.

The Worthing Sentinel.
Article published in April and May 2008.

Worthing Herald and Gazette.
Article published in May 2008.

The Worthing Argus.
Article published in May 2008.

The West Sussex Gazette.
Article published in May 2008.